The
Snowman
Who Went for a Walk

The
Snowman
Who Went for a Walk

by Mira Lobe
illustrated by Winfried Opgenoorth
translated by Peter Carter

The copyright notice and Cataloging in Publication information
are to be found on the last page.

William Morrow and Company
New York   1984

A snowman stood in a garden
in front of a house. There was
nothing special about him.
He was just an ordinary winter
snowman.

Inside the house it was warm. The
family sat in the dining room, drinking
tea and eating cookies left over from
Christmas. Liza went to the window and
breathed on the frosted glass. She made
a little peephole and peered through it.
Poor snowman, she thought, *he must be
very cold. I'll take him a cup of tea and
warm him up.*

Liza ran into the garden, gave the snowman a drink of tea, then hurried back inside the house. The snowman was very surprised. In his tummy there was a warm, creeping, crawling feeling, and in his snowy head there was a warm, creeping, crawling feeling, too. *Goodness,* he thought, *I'm not an ordinary snowman anymore. I am glowing inside!*

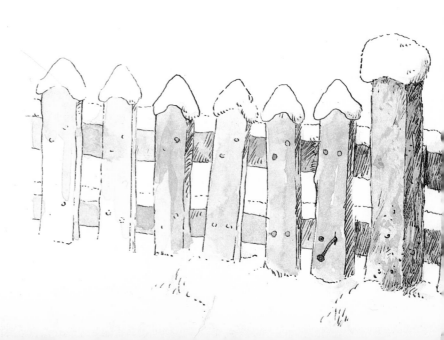

"It's because of the tea Liza gave me." He chuckled. "Why, I am not just a snowman, I am a glowman!" Then he thought, *A glowing man is a going man, so I must go.* He heaved up his great snowy feet and stamped down the garden path. At the gate he turned and waved to Liza. But Jack Frost had frozen up the peephole, and no one inside the house saw the snowman leave, so he wandered off into the town.

The snowman bumped into a
lamp post. "Gosh!" he said. His
old hat fell off and rolled away.
"Golly!" cried the snowman.
A boy brought the hat back.
"Thank you," said the snowman,
"but I don't think the town is the
right place for me. I don't want
to turn into a gollyman-goshman.
I must go where there are no
lamp posts for me to bump into."
"Then you must go to the countryside,"
said the boy, and he kindly showed the snowman the way.

The snowman plodded on his snowfeet
from the town into the countryside. The
fields and meadows were glittering white
and deep in snow. "How pretty," said the
snowman as he looked around him. Just
then a crow flew over the snowman and
perched on his old hat.

"What are you doing in my clover field?" croaked the crow. "What is a clover field?" asked the snowman. "In summer," said the crow, "all the field is green and the clover has red flowers." "How beautiful that must be," said the snowman. "I must stay here and then I can be a snowman-glowman-crowman."

"Oh, I don't think you can do that,"
squawked the crow. "In summer
snowmen melt and turn into water."
"Melt!" cried the snowman. "Gosh
and golly, then I would be a no-man.
This clover field is not the place
for me. I must find a place where
summer never comes." The crow
wagged its beak. "You must go to
the north where the polar bears live."
"Is it far away?" sighed the snowman.
"Very far, Mister Snowman," said the crow.
"The best way for you to go would be on
an ice floe. They are in the river now."
The crow flew to the river and the snowman
stumped after him. "There's one," said
the snowman, and he jumped onto it.
"Good-bye," called the crow. "Have a
good journey over the sea. Now you are a
snowman-glowman-crowman-floeman!"

The snowman sailed down the river on his ice floe. He passed fields and woods, villages and towns, and went under bridges until he came to the open sea. Far across the sea he journeyed, and farther still, and farther—always heading north.

And now, if you want to know
whether the snowman reached
the land of the polar bears, the
answer is yes, he did. I know
because a sea gull saw the
snowman-glowman-crowman-
floeman living happily with the
polar bears, and the gull told the
crow in the clover field, and the
crow told the boy who had given
the snowman his hat back, and
the boy told Liza, and Liza
told me!

10 9 8 7 6 5 4 3 2 1

Library of Congress Cataloging in Publication Data
Lobe, Mira.   The snowman who went for a walk.
    Translation of: Es ging ein Schneemann durch das Land.
    Summary: A snowman becomes mobile, and in his wanderings decides to seek a place where he can live and never melt. [1. Snowmen—Fiction]
I. Opgenoorth, Winfried, ill. II. Title.   PZ7.L7793Sn 1984   [E]   83-27298
ISBN 0-688-03865-4
ISBN 0-688-03866-2 (lib. bdg.)